A TEACHER'S GUIDE TO

W O R D S M I T H

By

Janie B. Cheaney

An overview, syllabus, and teaching suggestions

for the popular "Creative Writing Course For Young People"

Published by DGC Inc., Flemington, Missouri

Distributed by

See where learning takes you.

8786 Highway 21 • Melrose, FL 32666
(352) 475-5757 • Fax: (352) 475-6105
www.commonsensepress.com

Janie B. Cheaney taught her two children at home for twelve years, during which she also conducted creative writing classes for other homeschool students. Since 1990 she has seen her work published in magazines and literary journals. In addition she has worked with students in theater design and performance, and has written several plays for young people. Her first novel, *The Playmaker*, was published by Random House in 2000, followed by *The True Prince* in 2002. Mrs. Cheaney lives in the Ozarks of Missouri with her husband.

Rev 05/10
Printed 03/14

TEACHER 'S GUIDE TO *WORDSMITH*

WHAT THIS BOOK WILL NOT DO:

1. Teach comprehensive grammar. It's assumed that the student will know parts of speech and basic sentence structure. *Wordsmith* will, however, help him apply that knowledge.

2. Teach expository writing (reports, research papers, articles, etc.)--though the principles taught here will help with any kind of writing.

3. Produce an enthusiastic and prolific writer every time--but you may be surprised!

AN OVERVIEW OF WRITING DEVELOPMENT

If I could devise the ideal K-12 writing curriculum, the basic plan would look like this:

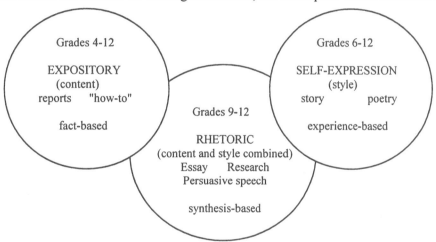

Notice that I wouldn't even address the subject of writing until fourth grade. Until then, most children have enough to do just learning to read and make letters. Of course, some take more naturally to writing than others, and that's fine: if they want to scribble stories as soon as they know how to spell their names, let them. But *making* children write stories and essays while they're still trying to learn cursive letters only amounts to a lot of heartache with little tangible gain. If you happen to be pulling your hair out over a second-grader's lack of composition skills, RELAX! Concentrate on reading instead. Read to them as much or more than they read to themselves: let the patterns of good literature fill their heads before asking for literature from their pencils.

Around fourth grade, or maybe even fifth, a child can move naturally from reading to writing. At this age the emphasis should be on content--*what* they write, not necessarily *how*, as long as they are producing complete sentences and reasonably coherent paragraphs. Also, their writing should be mostly fact-based--reports on what they read or what they do. There's a lot of interest these days in probing the emotions of young children: getting them to express how they feel about things. Of course, young children have feelings, but I don't think they are equipped to analyze them yet, and don't always feel comfortable doing it. Most elementary age children are interested in learning facts, not pondering or agonizing over them.

But this stage doesn't last. I've taught writing to upper-elementary grades and junior-high grades, back to back, and the contrast is striking. The younger class may contain woolgatherers and cut-ups, but if I am halfway interesting their attention is directed at me. Once they cross that line into junior high, their attention is directed sideways--all of a sudden they're more interested in each other than in me! This is the age when kids start asking the question: Who am I? You may not hear it in so many words, but when your daughter wails that she can't do anything right, or your son demands more privileges, that's the basic question they're exploring. They begin to look to their peers for answers, judging what kind of person they are by the responses they get from others. That's why I consider the grades 6-8 the optimum time for learning self-expression through writing. Not only *can* they do it now, but they *need* to do it now.

Wordsmith is written for students at the "Who Am I?" stage, but before returning to them, allow me to address the last circle briefly: Rhetoric. These days that word carries a sense of empty speech: sounds good, means little. But true rhetoric is a noble accomplishment, and I consider it the ultimate goal of teaching composition, in high school and beyond. Rhetoric is simply presenting the writer's point of view in a logical and forceful manner. It balances reason with passion and brings together the two sides of our nature. If students can clearly and winningly express a reasonable point of view, in writing, on a variety of subjects that mean something to them, I would call their education a success.

WHAT THIS BOOK WAS DESIGNED TO DO:

Creative writing, in the simplest terms, is **expressing oneself**: communicating what is inside to the world outside. Expository writing is from the head; creative writing is from the heart.

Why is this important? After all, most school assignments are of the expository type: factual and objective. In an information age, the demand will increase for articulate writers who can communicate information clearly, without artistic frills or "creative" flourishes. So why bother with creative writing at all?

The distinction between head and heart is not as clear-cut as it may appear. Human beings are integrated beings; head and heart are made to work together. The most memorable non-fiction is not dry, but charged with life and emotional appeal. The best fiction deals in concrete incident and detail, not vague flights of fancy. The major principles addressed in this book apply to both types of writing:

> **Use the tools of language (vocabulary and syntax) to your advantage.**
> **Bring your subject into sharp focus.**
> **Anchor your writing in concrete detail; don't generalize.**

Creative writing is a good place to start learning these principles, because your student has all the materials he needs close at hand--language and experience. He will be starting where he is.

No one is born knowing how to write. Though some are gifted with exceptional literary talent, even the most naturally gifted young writer must learn the craft in order to write well. Writing is a craft before it rises to the level of an art. This is an important distinction: art may be the purview of the gifted, but a craft is simply an acquired skill. To learn a craft, you gather the tools, learn to use them, and then practice your technique. Because all humans possess the tools-- the great gift of language--anybody, with practice, can learn to express himself or herself in written words.

Wordsmith is designed to help young people sharpen their language skills, then put those skills to imaginative use. A motivated student could work through the book without much supervision, but it's a sad fact that many students are *not* motivated to write. Josh may be able to take apart his clock radio and put it back together so that it actually works better than it did before, but when faced with a blank page he can only despair of tomorrow. Kelli may be a math whiz and a precocious reader, but constructing more than two paragraphs seems beyond her. Writing is simply hard work.

Why should writing be any more difficult for students than figuring areas or labeling flower diagrams? Why is it that many of them just can't seem to get started? My theory is that the subject throws too wide a net. The problem, not just for children but for adults too, is not of scarcity but of glut. Rather than having too little to write about, we all have experienced more than any book could hold, and our language contains hundreds of thousands of words to express that experience. The purpose of *Wordsmith* is to help children pare this huge task down to a manageable size. The burden of learning falls mainly on them, but you, the teacher, have an important role to play as encourager, sounding board, critic and sometimes conscience ("Where's that writing assignment you were supposed to turn in today?"). You are also a fellow traveler--the best teachers learn right along with their students.

THE *WORDSMITH* APPROACH

Part One concentrates on word usage. Much of this is familiar ground to children who have studied grammar since second grade. Rather than the familiar drill about what the parts of speech are, the emphasis is on how to use and expand one's vocabulary to advantage. Special emphasis is given to nouns and verbs as the "building blocks" of language, to choosing effective adjectives, to the proper use of adverbs, to the function of prepositions, and to the pronoun-antecedent relationship.

Part Two is concerned with sentences--strong vs. weak constructions, active and passive voice, and how to achieve sentence variety in a paragraph. This section in no way covers the subject of sentence construction, but is intended to introduce new possibilities inherent in it. The subject-switching "formula" on page 29, for example, is a useful tool for breaking old patterns.

In **Part Three** the student leaves exercises behind and tackles longer writing assignments. This is where adult involvement is especially helpful, because few youngsters are apt to voluntarily do all the revision and rewriting necessary to produce their best work. Each division of Part Three contains some practice work, followed by at least two formal assignments. In general, the first of these assignments will be based on the student's personal experience; the last will require the transfer of that experience to an imaginary situation. Reluctant writers are more the rule than the exception, but don't be surprised if an occasional project fires a child's imagination or engages his heart. Sometimes a simple device, like changing a point of view or revising an opening sentence, can open up new worlds to a young mind. This does happen--I've seen it happen in the most unliterary children.

If, by the end of the book, you still have a reluctant writer on your hands, remember that not all of us are called to produce novels or stories or magazine articles. Almost certainly he or she will have learned something about using written language, a basic and irreplaceable skill that seems to be eroding in our electronic age. My goal is to clear up some of the mystery and help students draw from and express the rich source material they carry with them--their own experience.

But remember, practice is the key to learning almost anything. *Wordsmith* tries to teach some helpful pointers and guidelines, but no child will become a writer just by working through the course. The only way to learn to write well is to do lots of writing. I hope this book will be only a start.

HOW TO USE *WORDSMITH*

The course may be completed in three to nine months, depending on the student's age, aptitude, interest, and workload. The syllabus paces the work through one 36-week school year, including at least a little practice every day except Friday (with a few exceptions). Student assignments are boxed. All suggestions are merely that--you may copy them as is into your schedule book or adapt them to fit your needs.

The review quizzes are included to remind the student of material covered weeks before. Since there is no one right answer to any of the questions, grading is subjective. I would grade mostly on the basis of effort. Discuss the student's answers but correct only the ones that you think are especially weak. I've included some sentence and paragraph rewrites at the end of this guide, but only for the sake of comparison. My answers are by no means the "right" ones.

While working through the course, be on the lookout for good literature that illustrates the principles taught, such as using strong verbs or incorporating lots of sensory detail. This helps students realize that the rules they are learning are not just *my* idea--all good writers use them!

NOTE: Throughout this Guide I use "he" as a generic pronoun, simply because it's easier and more resonant than the awkward compounds he/she or himself/herself. Style won over social conscience.

ABOUT REVISION

Revision is an inexact science; most writers end up trusting their instincts as to what "sounds" good to them. Experienced instincts can often be trusted, but a beginner needs some guidance in making intelligent choices--a responsibility which will likely fall to you. Don't be surprised if your own beginner resents the intrusion. "I have to say it my own way," is the usual line, and the more serious a young writer is about his work, the more sincere his protest will be. However, while it's true that every writer must develop his own style, that development does not occur entirely within the feverish workings of his own imagination.

Tell your budding young artist that every writer, even (name a favorite author here) has to subject his or her work to criticism and apply the editor's suggestions. You may not consider yourself a good judge of literature, but you've read more than a 12-year-old and probably have better instincts than you think. In the first months, you as teacher will play a large role in the revision process, but by the end of the course the student should be taking more of that responsibility on himself. If he doesn't like your "interference," reassure him that greater artistic freedom will be his down the road, as long as he uses certain basic, proven and time-honored principles.

HOW TO REVISE

The easiest approach is to read the paper first for spelling, punctuation and grammatical errors, mark them with the dreaded red ink, and require the student to correct them before going further. I'll admit, I've recommended this sequence in the past because it gives the teacher some confidence that she knows what she's doing. But perhaps the student's confidence is more important. I firmly believe that the rules should be followed and mechanics are important, but the first goal of this course is to encourage young people to write. Too much red ink on a paper can knock the wind out of them before they've even made a start!

So concentrate on content first. This involves how well the student expressed his thoughts, how those thoughts were arranged, where the impact seems weaker than it should have been, where another choice of words, more detail, or a direct quote might have helped. My three rules for revision are these:

1. First, find something to compliment, even if it's only the fact that the left margin is straight. Every small step forward, every attempt at improvement should be recognized.
2. Avoid the word "But--". Children develop an uncanny sense of where that word is going to fall. A sensitive writer will wait for it, as a condemned man waits before the firing squad. No matter how many compliments you've showered on a composition, as long as the student knows this is an editing session he'll be waiting for that word. So make a conscious effort to avoid it. Instead of, "Your opening sentence is good, but this description seems weak," you could say, "I'm glad you mentioned the dress. Is there anything else you could say about it?" Instead of, "I like the way you described the race, but you could have a stronger verb here," say, "Can you think of a better action word here than 'went'?" Questions like this help to get students involved in the revision process, and that's what you want anyway. Your goal is to teach them to do it, not to become their permanent editor.
3. Don't try to fix everything. Don't make that paper bleed red ink--it can be very discouraging to a tender heart who doesn't enjoy writing anyway. Focus on one or two problems, and work on correcting those. During the months of writing adventures ahead of you, you should have time to address the rest.

While we're on the subject of editing, several symbols are standard in the publishing industry and in the schools. It's a good idea to learn and use them, if you don't already:

ꞁ	Delete word or short phrase	∩	Reverse letter or word order
(‿ℯ)	Delete longer phrase or sentence	ℛ	Capitalize
⊙⊙	Delete or change circled punctuation	ℓ	Lower-case
¶	Start new paragraph	put "here ∧	Insert (letter, word, phrase, or sentence)

Once the paper is edited and corrected to the satisfaction of both the teacher and the writer, it's time to make a final copy, typed or neatly written. Now is the time to correct the technical errors: misspelled words should go on a list; persistent grammatical errors can become the subject of a short remedial lesson. At least some assignments should be typed. Typing just *looks* different from script, and it can give a student a fresh and startling view of his own work. Typing is also one of the most useful skills any child will ever learn--an almost indispensable skill in our increasingly computer-oriented world.

A computer or word processor of course makes the revision process much easier by eliminating the tedious copy work. Most families now own at least one computer. If your student does not, either for financial or philosophical reasons, he can learn to write quite well without one. After all, most of the world's great literature was written before computers were even imagined. It's not hardware but heart that counts.

Student critiques--evaluations by classmates or siblings--can be helpful. Some students may try a little harder if they know they are writing for their peers, and at the end of this guide I'll give some suggestions for setting up a writer's club for that very purpose. But peer review at this age means "amateur assessment." It's no substitute for honest evaluation by an experienced reader: yourself!

SUGGESTED PLAN OF STUDY FOR WORDSMITH -36 WEEKS

It's a good idea to keep all *Wordsmith* writing assignments together as long as you continue this course. Invest in a three-ring binder or a sturdy portfolio with pockets. This will make it easier to check assignments against guidelines in the book, or compare current assignments with previous ones, or rewrite pieces written weeks earlier.

WEEK l.
Monday

```
Read and be ready to discuss the Introduction,pp. i-ii.
```

If you have a print of *Washington Crossing the Delaware,* perhaps in a history text or art book, it may be helpful to look at it with the student and pay close attention to the composition. Notice how the line and light emphasize the figure of Washington, and speculate on what the effect might have been if the artist had highlighted some other part of the picture and left Washington in the shadows. The point of this illustration is to introduce some of the possibilities of creative writing-- not just getting suitable words on paper, but *choosing* words to build to a climax, make a point, provoke a thought or a laugh. There are at least as many dimensions to writing as there are to painting, and literature can be as "pictorial" as visual art.

Tuesday-Wednesday

```
Write an essay about two double-spaced pages long
          entitled, "What I Did Last Summer."
```

("Two *pages!* I can't write two whole pages!") This topic is almost guaranteed to produce a boring paper, and that's exactly what is intended. If summer is too far away, assign another topic equally broad, such as "School," or "I Like Sports." Give no guidelines, and when the assignment is completed, make no corrections other than spelling and grammatical errors. Keep this paper in the creative writing folder--periodically he'll take it out for specific revisions. By the time he's finished the course, the student should be favorably impressed with the progress he's made.

Thursday

```
Read pages 1-3 and complete Exercise 1-A.
```

WEEK 2. By this time in the student's career, there should be no confusion about what nouns are. The goal in this section is to emphasize the use of specific, concrete nouns over general ones.

Monday
Discuss the material on pages 1-3 to make sure the student understands it, then go over his list of nouns. If he was not able to come up with at least five for every general noun, do some brainstorming together, and list as many as you can think of until you run out of room. Then look at the example for Exercise 1-B on page 4 and point out how dramatically a concrete noun can change the meaning. If he seems uncertain of what to do, collaborate on writing three versions of sentence # 1.

NOTE: It may be necessary to explain what "concrete" means in this context--not the stuff of sidewalks and swimming pools, but "concrete" in the sense of being definite and solid.

Finish Exercise 1-B, pp. 4-6.

Tuesday
Read through his sentences together. Did he choose specific nouns to replace the general ones? Does the subsequent action follow logically from the changes he made? It may be interesting to choose one of the sentences and develop a little plot from each variation.

Look at Exercise 1-C together and notice the examples. It wouldn't hurt to limit our use of these two words in speaking as well as writing. I'm especially lazy about the word "people," and have recently made an effort to substitute " Americans," "senior citizens," or "pseudo-intellectual freethinkers" as the situation demands. Fuzzy language means fuzzy thinking!

Finish exercise 1-C, p. 6.

Wednesday
Here are some appropriate substitute nouns for the sentences in Exercise C. Notice that I used a prepositional phrase and a few adjectives, but it's not necessary to comment on them yet.

```
1. wise words, stories, proverbs, principles, truths
2. children, of my friends, grownups, Americans
3. teacher, performer, teenager, octogenarian
4. art objects, hobby and craft supplies, books (or all these)
5. crustacean, spider, little brother, praying mantis
6. packing crates, toys, ropes and extension cords
7. (You could have a lot of fun with this one.)
```

Sometimes the object in question is so broad that only "thing" or "person" will cover it. I'm not saying these words should never be used; I'm merely suggesting that they should not be used thoughtlessly.

Talk over the room description assignment on page 7. Emphasize that this should be double-spaced. Students who have trouble forming this habit should mark every other line of the paper with an "X" as a reminder not to write on that line. Be clear that the paragraph will be re-copied after corrections are made, and mention that if he doesn't know what to name certain objects in the room, he should ask.

> Write a paragraph describing your living room as
> defined in Exercise 1-D on p.7.

Thursday
Now for the revision. (Reread "About Revision" on p. 4 of this guide to fortify yourself for the task.) Ask the student to read the description aloud, correcting any spelling or punctuation errors as he spots them. Then go through the paragraph together and circle every noun. Look at each one to see if any could be made more concrete. Certainly a "white wall" is more specific than a "wall," but concentrate on nouns, not adjectives. "Paneling" or "brickwork" might do for "wall," if either applies. Before changing *all* the nouns, read the "Caveat" on page 7 and discuss which general nouns, if any, might remain in the paragraph--or where a general noun might even be better. By now the spaces between the written lines should have some corrections in them, especially if you caught spelling errors that the student missed. If you feel you've mauled the nouns enough, and both of you are satisfied with the result, ask for a neat copy with all corrections made. The final copy should also be double-spaced, because we'll be making further corrections in a few weeks.

Be sure to keep all final copies of these assignments in a portfolio or loose-leaf binder.

The "More Practice" assignment is up to your discretion: if you feel more practice is needed, or if the student is eager to try it (yes, it's possible), ask him to write the paragraph over the weekend or on Monday. Very resistant writers should not be forced to do too much at the beginning; allow the regular exercises and assignments to build confidence first. Week 6 in this guide is set aside for review; you may wish to save the "More Practice" assignment for then. The "Just For Fun" exercise would obviously fit very well with a science or nature class, and can be done with a younger sibling. Or even yourself--can *you* name all the varieties of trees in your yard?

WEEK 3. The importance of building a good vocabulary of nouns and verbs can't be over-emphasized. This week we focus on verbs.

Monday

> Read pp. 8 and complete exercise 2-A.

Tuesday
Discuss the word choices the student made yesterday and comment on the verbs you especially like. Then read directions and example for Exercise 2-B on p. 9. Once he fully understands the exercise, give him the following assignment:

> Finish exercise 2-B on p. 9. Then read page 10

Wednesday
Discuss the three sentences about Jenna on page 10. The point should be obvious, but make sure the student sees how much work a well-chosen verb can do. Exercise 2-C on p. 10 can be a joint project. Once you've chosen verbs that show how satisfied Sally is, choose another set to show her as angry, or excited. Refer to the verb list in the appendix for help and, if you have a thesaurus, get it out and demonstrate how to use it. (Sometimes a thesaurus is not as helpful as I thought it would be--that's why I compiled the verb list.)

```
Rewrite the three paragraphs in Exercise 2-D on p. 11
to show a definite mood in the characters portrayed.
```

Thursday
It might be fun for you to rewrite your own versions of the three paragraphs (or just make a list of verbs for each one). Let the student read his versions, then read yours, and guess what emotion is expressed in each case. For example:

```
Ivan stalked across the street. "Did you see that van?" he
demanded. (anger, indignation)
```

Other possibilities:
```
1. darted, gulped (surprise)
   scurried, stuttered (anxiety)
2. eased, whispered, glided, rested (awe)
   grabbed, snapped, strode, slammed (anger)
3. tiptoed, peered, faltered (nervousness)
   strutted, glared, barked (indignation)
```

The "Caveat" on page 11 reassures the student that he needn't swear off neutral verbs altogether, but encourages him to be on the lookout for interesting verbs, which he can add to the list on p. 90. This is a great way to "cultivate that garden."

The "More Practice" assignment on p. 11 is again up to your discretion; you may save it until the Week 6 review, or combine it with Exercise 3 as an assignment. The "Just For Fun" exercise might be an interesting group activity, it you have a rather uninhibited group!

The section on adverbs is actually a supplement to verbs, since the idea of concentrating on strong, high-energy verbs is reinforced. The main point I want to stress about adverbs is not to use too many, especially of the "-ly" type. That's one sure mark of the overeager writing student.

```
Read p. 12 and do your best to think of verbs that can
be substituted for the verb-adverb combinations in the
          exercise. For help, check the verb list.
```

WEEK 4. This week we'll be talking about modifiers, specifically adjectives and adverbs. Before we begin, it may help to brush up on syntax (sentence construction).

Nouns and verbs are the building blocks of any language. To illustrate this point, I sometimes bring a set of wooden building blocks to class. The large oblong blocks are designated as nouns (one color) and verbs (another color). These form the base or foundation of a sentence. There are two basic sentence foundations--only two. They are subject-verb, and subject-verb-object (a slight variation is the subject-linking verb-compliment form). The subject and object of a sentence is *always* a noun, or a noun substitute (like a pronoun or gerund), and *every* sentence must contain a verb. No exceptions. Everything else--adjectives, adverbs, prepositional phrases, clauses, etc.-- will modify a noun or a verb. To "modify" means to qualify, locate, number, or otherwise describe the word modified. That's syntax in a nutshell: nouns and verbs make the basic sentence; everything else modifies.

Personally, I find the subject of grammar immensely intriguing. Consider how many toddlers can speak in sentences so complex many of us wouldn't know how to diagram them. How do they gain that inherent knowledge of syntax? Whether inborn or learned, without grammar we could communicate only by signals; abstract concepts would be impossible to explain or to understand.

Monday
If there were some blanks left in the exercise on p. 12, go over the verb list on p. 90 together and fill them. There *will* be at least one appropriate verb for each example, I promise.

Sentence diagramming (once called "parsing") has fallen out of favor, but no exercise better demonstrates the logic of language. A diagram is a picture of how words in a sentence relate to each other, making an abstract concept visible. Here are diagrams of three sentences, each containing an adverb:

```
Who put this book here?
Reed gave a memorable speech today.
Mr. McBride cheerfully shared his memories.
```

When parsing a sentence, locate the subject and the verb first, then decide what the modifiers are and where they go. Any word that tells **when, where, how** or **how much** is an adverb, and usually modifies the verb. In the first example above, "here" tells **where**. In the second, "today" tells **when**. In the second, "cheerfully" tells **how**. All three adverbs modify the verb. Adverbs that tell **how much** usually modify other modifiers, as in these examples:

```
Vernon walked very softly to the door. ("very" modifies an adverb)
Margo was wearing this totally awesome leather jacket.
        ("totally" modifies an adjective.)
```

If this is not getting through, try to find some adverbs in a book or magazine article that you or your student is reading. You don't have to diagram the sentences, but note whether the adverb tells when, where, how, or how much.

Now we move on to adjectives, which are fortunately easier to understand.

```
        Read p. 13 and complete exercise 4-A.
```

If you have a rather unobservant student, make sure he notices the "list of adjectives to choose from" at the end of exercise 4-A.

Tuesday

Review exercise 4-A with the student and be sure to compliment any adjectives he included that were not on the list. Together, each of you might try to come up with one more original adjective that would be appropriate in each case--you have hundreds to choose from!

Now look at the first paragraph about camp on p. 14. All of the underlined words are merely variations of the word "good" and say nothing particular about the nouns they modify. Ask which of the two paragraphs the student prefers and don't be surprised if he chooses the first one. This is the way a youngster might speak if asked to describe a memorable experience: "It was really *awesome,* you know?" Point out again that it's okay to talk that way, but writing must be more precise. Many children will have to be reminded of this principle over and over.

Exercise 4-B is designed to help a young writer distinguish adjectives of *quality*. For some this may be difficult. Be sure the student understands that we're looking for descriptive words, not just words of approval or disapproval, like "bad," "awful," "fantastic," or "wonderful." Keep a thesaurus handy.

```
            Finish Exercise 4-B on pp. 14-15.
```

Wednesday

Discuss the student's answers for Exercise 4-B, then ask him to fill in the synonyms required by Exercise 4-C. You should be available to help, if necessary. Some suggested synonyms are

```
sad: gloomy, depressed, grief-stricken, moody, distressed
mean: cruel, petty, vindictive, unkind, ruthless
lively: bouncy, cheerful, frisky, spirited, excitable
fearful: cautious, nervous, anxious, frightened, terrified
```

Look over Exercise 4-D and make sure the student knows what to do.

```
       Finish the sentences in exercise 4-D, pp. 16-17.
```

Thursday

Check the work on Exercise 4-D. Does the quote in each case make sense with the adjective? Be encouraging and praise any combinations that seem especially apt or striking to you. In this type of exercise, no word choice is *wrong,* unless it's misspelled, but remember to strive for clarity in writing--the more precise, the better.

Now note the two caveats on p. 17. Most children err on the side of too few descriptive words rather than too many, but the warning is included here lest they conclude that more adjectives make better writing. One mark of a novice writer is loading up his prose with adjectives and adverbs in this mistaken assumption. Some best-selling authors suffer from the same delusion. All this accomplishes, in my view, is to suffocate the reader.

The second warning boils down to this: spoken language is often imprecise, but written language should never be. Words such as "weird", "gross" and "awesome" have become too broad in meaning to be of much use in writing. If your student still has trouble understanding why the use of colloquial words is unwise, just tell him it's because I said so.

Finally, discuss the restaurant review on p. 18. If your local paper runs restaurant reviews, you may want to substitute a recent review for the *Wordsmith* example. (If you find your mouth watering as you underline the adjectives, you may end up having lunch there!) I've heard it said that one can judge what a society deems important by the number of words available to describe it. Did you ever realize how many adjectives we can use to describe food? If time and interest permits, make a list of adjectives that may be used to describe different types of food: crunchy, savory, salty, spicy, creamy, crisp, pungent, tangy, etc. The review should be finished over the weekend.

> Write a restaurant review according to directions in
> Exercise 4-E, pp. 17-18.

WEEK 5

Monday

Ask the student to read his review aloud, marking any corrections that may have been missed in the first proofreading. Both of you may notice that many of the sentences start the same way: "The service was..." "The atmosphere was..." This is a problem, but we'll address it later; for now, concentrate on the adjectives. If it seems to you that they could be sharper, get out the thesaurus and look up synonyms. When both of you are reasonably satisfied with the word choices and all corrections have been made, put the review aside for a few days. For more work on adjectives, combine the "Just for Fun" activity on p. 18 with the following exercise.

> Read about prepositions, on pp. 19-20. Rewrite the
> sentences in Exercise 5-A, pp. 20-21.

The student is asked to read the material on his own, but if he's never encountered prepositions he may need help in understanding the material and rewriting the first sentence in Exercise 5-A.

Tuesday

Read the rewritten sentences to make sure the student understands what prepositions are and how they work. Remember our "syntax in a nutshell": prepositional phrases are an addition to our collection of modifiers. The diagram on p. 19 is an approximation. Prepositional phrases are usually diagrammed like this:

> Write one original sentence for each of the six
> prepositional phrases listed in Exercise 5-B, p. 21.
> Then rewrite each sentence once as directed.

Wednesday

Read the student's original sentences and compliment his work--that is, if you can! Now, take out that restaurant review and read it one more time. Do you see any prepositional phrases that could be moved around for variety's sake, or could such a phrase be added at the beginning of a sentence? Avoid such colorless phrases as "all in all" and "in the long run," but consider where a prepositional phrase might actually help clarify a statement as well as add variety. Try to add at least two prepositional phrases to the review.

```
Type or write a neat copy of your revised restaurant
         review, and proofread.  Read pp. 22-23.
```

Thursday

Discuss the previous day's reading about pronouns and make sure the student understands what an antecedent is. Read over the corrections of the "pillow fight" story and note the many different ways I used to identify the antecedent. Unclear antecedents are a problem that pops up even in the writing of professional authors, and it's not always easily solved. A writer may even have to resort to the blatantly obvious, as in: "Ron was jealous of Paul because of his (Paul's) many successes." My purpose in this section is to make the student aware of the problem and suggest a few solutions.

```
Correct the paragraph in Exercise 6 on p. 23 to make
   the antecedents clear. Corrections may be written
between the lines or in the margins; you don't have to
              rewrite the paragraph.
```

WEEK 6. Depending on the student's progress, this might be a good time to stop and review.

Monday

```
Reread pp. 1-11 and do the "More Practice" exercise on
             p. 7 (if you haven't already).
```

Tuesday

```
Take out the assignment you wrote five weeks ago about
your summer.  Read it over carefully, paying particular
   attention to the nouns and verbs you used.  Mark at
  least two nouns and two verbs that could be made more
   specific or vigorous. Do the "More Practice" exercise
                     on p. 11.
```

Wednesday

```
Reread pp. 12-24.  Write five original sentences, each
           containing two prepositional phrases.
```

Thursday

Talk over the summertime composition and suggest any other general nouns that might be more concrete or weak verbs that could be stronger. Now, what adjectives were used? Does "good" or "great" or "wonderful" appear more than once? How could these qualities be better defined? Mark the words that could stand some improvement, then write the suggested improvements in the margins.

Take a few moments to review prepositions and their function. If the student can't tell you what the function is, look at the section on prepositions again. Their purpose is to turn a noun into a modifier, and the way they are diagrammed depends on whether they modify a noun or a verb.

Try these sentences again:

> Reed gave a memorable speech at Toastmaster's Club today.
> Cheerfully, Mr. McBride shared memories of his childhood.

"At Toastmasters Club" acts as an adverb because it tells **where**. "Of his childhood," however, tells what kind of memories Mr. McBride is sharing; it describes a noun, so it serves as an adjective.

Let me reassure you that I don't believe you have to master all the grammatical concepts of English usage in order to become a good writer. But some notion of sentence structure is necessary for effective writing. If the student has a good grasp of these concepts already, you may of course skip the whole diagramming practice and go on to the next page.

> Read your summer composition one more time and review your word choices. Are there any more you would like to change? Is there any misunderstanding about to what or whom your pronouns refer? Mark any further change you would like to make and keep the composition.

WEEK 7. Sentence construction is a vast and complicated subject, but an essential one. The sentence is the basic unit of language, and the most important element of good writing.

Monday

> Study Section 1 of Part 2, pp. 25-27. Be sure to underline the subject and circle the verb in each sentence in the first paragraph on p. 26.

Tuesday
Discuss the reading from yesterday. Some 6th-8th graders grasp the principles of sentence construction easily. A surprising number of them, however, lack a basic understanding of how

sentences are put together. For their sake, Section 1 is included. It's important to be sure your student understands this material before proceeding, so take some time to discuss it. If he had trouble locating the subjects and verbs in the first paragraph, drawing some diagrams might be helpful:

We all speak in complex sentence patterns every day. The first sentence in the fifth paragraph on page 26 seems straightforward and simple, but could you diagram it? It looks like this:

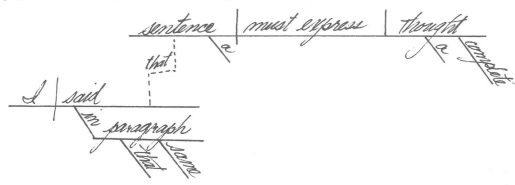

(If your student sometimes doubts your qualifications as a teacher of English, you may wish to draw this diagram and awe him into silence for a few blessed seconds.)

Fragments are common errors, and often a bad habit that's hard to break. Those who make a habit of writing with sentence fragments may justify them as a matter of style. That's why the paragraphs at the bottom of p. 26 and top of p. 27 are worth reading again. If this restriction presents a problem to your free-spirited author, point out that fragments are like the special tools that an artist or mechanic can use *only* after he's mastered the basic techniques. And even then, they are to be used sparingly.

> Read pp. 27-28 and complete Exercise 2-A. Then rewrite the description of your living room according to Exercise 2-B.

Wednesday
The subjects and verbs of the room description in Exercise 2-A should be identified as follows: 1) room/has; 2) It/has; 3) I/have; 4) room/has; 5) dresser/is; 6) I/like. Go over each sentence of the room description on p. 27-28 and note how the sentences were improved.

Now read the revised living room description and compliment any improvements. (Almost any alteration of an "It has" or "There is" structure is an improvement.) Make any obvious corrections, but don't do a thorough revision yet. If the rewrite was difficult, explain that the transformation techniques we'll look at today should make the job easier. Read the material on pp. 28-30 together, and if the transforming idea seems difficult to grasp, help with rewriting the first sentences in Exercises 2-C and 2-D.

> Complete exercises 2-C and 2-D on pp. 29 and 30.

Thursday
Check the student's work and make any helpful suggestions. Here are some possible sentence rewrites.

C 1. A four-poster bed dominates one corner of my room.
2. A broken handle disfigures the cup.
3. A huge oak tree shades our back yard.
4. An irritating bark made me want to kick the Chihuahua.
5. A huge swimming pool draws crowds to Pride Park.

D 1. A fountain splashes noisily in the park.
2. Four children complete the family.
3. A hat with an ostrich plume sat on the shelf.
4. A giant lurked on the other side of the hill.
5. Three office buildings stand at Main and Strather.

I should reiterate that there is nothing incorrect about starting a sentence with the word "there." Alert readers will discover several clauses or sentences beginning with "there" throughout this book--one of them in this paragraph! But avoiding "there is" for the duration of the course is like swearing off candy bars while training for the Olympics. The only thing seriously wrong with candy bars is the eater's overindulgence, and certain word patterns can be overindulged as well. Avoiding them for a season is a disciplinary measure.

I've found "The Formula" to be a useful tool for encouraging children to break settled habits of sentence formation. But be aware that its use is not absolutely guaranteed to produce the best sentences every time. Only practice will give the writer a "feel" for using various sentence patterns effectively.

> In your summer vacation composition, find and rewrite
> two sentences that could be transformed according to
> "the Formula."

WEEK 8

Monday
Read the sentences your student "transformed" last week. If he's getting sick and tired of this summer vacation story, counsel just a little more patience. It will pay off.

If possible, locate a short passage in a book or magazine that contains both active and passive sentences. After reading about verb "voice" on pp. 30-31, ask the student to locate the passive sentences in the book passage. If he has trouble distinguishing between active and passive, he may need some help with the sentence transformations in exercise 2-E.

Look at sentence # 1 together. This is a passive sentence. An attempt to transform it to active will quickly reveal that the writer must invent a subject; the sentence as it is does not supply one. An obvious rewrite is "The audience wildly applauded the symphony's performance." Warn your student that he may have to invent a few more subjects in the course of the exercise.

```
Reread the section on active-passive transformations
    (pp. 30-31) and complete Exercise 2-E, pp. 31-32.
```

Tuesday

If the student followed *all* the directions in Exercise 2-E, some words in each preferred sentence should be circled. I asked if he could detect a pattern, and this is it: in most cases, the subject is the word or group of words which seem to be the most "important." It's vital for the reader to understand early on what the sentence is about; that's why the subject carries so much weight.

The rewritten sentences should read like this:

```
 1. The audience wildly applauded the symphony's performance.
 2. The race was finally finished by Randy.
 3. The mail is delivered later on Saturdays.
 4. E. A. Poe wrote "The Gold Bug."
 5. The volcano killed many island natives.
 6. Many are asking, "What can we do?"
 7. We often sweep our "little" faults under the rug.
 8. These are the times that try men's souls.
 9. A wise author is praised by his own works.
10. All babies are loved by Susan.
```

Together, read the active-passive comparisons on page 32. Do you agree with my judgment about which version is preferable? Discuss why or why not. If the student's understanding of verb voice seems a little shaky, try to find more examples of active and passive in a story or textbook.

```
Rewrite the paragraph in exercise 2-F, p. 32-33, to
make it more interesting.
```

Wednesday

The rewritten paragraph should demonstrate if the student has a firm grasp on sentence transformations. Ask him to read it out loud and evaluate his work. Is "has" or "have" used more than once? What happened to all the "It has" or "There is" sentences? What's the most colorful verb he used? For what it may be worth, here's my version:

```
        Red and gold, in the walls and on my Chinese silk
    bedspread, give my room a dramatic flair. My bed hangs
    from the ceiling on golden chains. Under the bed, a
    trap door opens to a heated pool in the basement. An
    entertainment system with wide-screen TV and a
    refrigerator well stocked with soda and ice cream
    contribute to the ideal place to relax with friends.
    Big glass doors open onto the balcony, where I can watch
    the sunset. My room is my castle.
```

For the rest of the week, the topic will be connecting and combining sentences. It's important to understand the distinction.

Connecting is simply joining one sentence to another, related sentence, either with a connecting word or with the proper punctuation. **Combining** is more difficult--it involves grafting part of one sentence into another, usually with some degree of revision. The next few pages may seem rather technical, and a student who is not especially well versed in English grammar will probably need help. Read over the material yourself to make sure you understand it, then be prepared to answer questions.

```
Read Section 3 ("Connections") on pp. 34-35.  Then take
out your summer story and find two sentence connections
                   you could make.
```

Thursday

We will be covering a lot of material rather quickly here, so make sure the student comprehends it all. Conjunctions may seem confusing, but that's probably because of the long, bulky names we have to use for such puny little words. The principle itself is simple. If necessary, demonstrate how the **coordinating conjunction** in the sentences below may be removed, resulting in two complete sentences.

```
Debbie left the party early, but Jerri stayed.
The Central High majorettes started the parade and the marching
    band followed.
```

This is not true of **subordinate conjunctions**, as we will see.

("Comma splices," or joining two complete sentences with a comma, is a common mistake even among adults who should know better. It drives me crazy. Don't do it!)

```
Read Section 4, pp. 35-37 and note with a question mark
            (?) anything you don't understand.
```

Friday

```
Take Review Quiz #1, pp. 95-96.
```

WEEK 9

Monday

Notice that Review Quiz #1 concerns material covered in Part One. We haven't been talking about vocabulary and word choice lately, but the subject will come up again in Part Three, so the quiz serves as a reminder.

Relative pronouns, participles and participial phrases are introduced in Section 4. By the age of ten most of us will have used these in everyday speech without the slightest idea what they are. I tried to explain as clearly as possible, but some students will need to read the material more than once. The whimsical illustration of "performing surgery" on one of the sentences may confuse more than it helps, if the student is rather literal-minded. Explain, if need be, that this is a word picture to help him understand what's going on (more on metaphors later in the book). A similar illustration is the "altered wedding dress." It may be helpful to diagram the examples given:

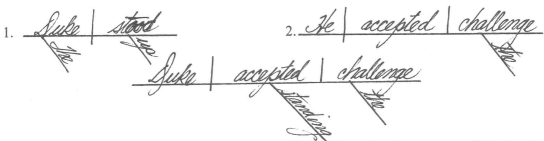

The diagrams illustrate how the verb in Sentence One is changed to become a modifier for the verb in Sentence Two.

When participles are placed too far from the words they modify, they are said to "dangle." That's the problem with the two sentences at the top of p. 37. (Be sure to tell your student; he'll be delighted to know what a dangling participle is.) Two possible rewrites are

```
Eddie had a wonderful view of the Canadian Rockies while riding in
     the observation car.
Singing their triumphant song, the maidens of Argon came out to
     meet the returning heroes.
```

```
          Reread pp. 35-37, then write two versions of sentences
                    #1-5 in Exercise 4-A on pp. 38-39.
```

Tuesday

```
          Write two versions of sentences #6-10 in Exercise 4-A,
                              pp. 39-40.
```

Wednesday
Check the rewritten sentences and make sure the student knows the difference between connections and combinations.

Together, notice the paragraph beginning, "Although we've done a lot of connecting work . . ." on p. 40. This makes an important point. A beginning writer should know that short sentences are fine, but they should be used for a purpose. As a writer begins to perceive how words and sentences can be arranged for effect, he's on his way to developing, half-unconsciously, the special patterns and peculiarities of language expression known as **style**. The average twelve-year-old has no perception of style as such, but when he decides for one word or phrase over another, trades a long sentence for two short ones or vice versa, moves the quotation from the end to the beginning of the paragraph, he's making style decisions.

As preparation for the next assignment, look at the ad copy together, and ask your child to underline the four sentence fragments. They are: "Comfort"; "Serenity"; "A unique retirement. . ."; "A relaxed, informal lifestyle . . ."

```
               Rewrite the ad in Exercise 4-B, p. 40.
```

Wednesday
In a magazine or newspaper, try to find a display ad with sentence fragments similar to the one on p. 40 (it shouldn't be too difficult). Read the ad the student rewrote yesterday, and discuss whether his version or the original version is more effective for *advertising*. Which do you think makes for

better literature? Why do you suppose many ads are written this way? Do you think the choppy style is overdone? (I'm not giving any right or wrong answers here; you decide.)

> Rewrite the paragraph in Exercise 4-C, p. 40, breaking
> up some of the long sentences into shorter ones.

Thursday

Read the rewritten paragraph together and note the sentences that were changed. Ask the student to explain *why* he shortened these particular sentences. He should have a reason other than, "It sounds better." *Why* does it sound better? Is this where he thinks the reader should sit up and take notice? Does the action call for a break at this point?

Review some of the rewritten sentences from pp. 38-40 and ask the student to identify some participial phrases, relative clauses and sentence connectors for you. Turn back a few pages and review active-passive transformations and the "super sentence" formula.

WEEK 10

Monday. Variety is the spice of good writing, but even variety is not everything. Some of the greatest prose ever written has depended on *similarity* for its effectiveness. If you think your student will be interested, call his attention to these two examples:

> Let us therefore boldly face the life of strife, resolute to do our duty well and manfully; resolute to uphold righteousness by deed and word; resolute to be both honest and brave, to serve high ideals with practical methods. (Theodore Roosevelt)

> . . .We shall fight on the beaches; we shall fight on the landing grounds, we shall fight in the fields and in the streets; we shall fight in the hills. We shall never surrender. . . . (Winston Churchill)

Are these passages effective and memorable? What makes them so? Obviously, repetition--but we've spent half our work on sentences exploring ways to avoid repetition!

By now, your student should be catching on to the fact that--while he must obey rules of spelling and grammar--there are almost no hard and fast rules of writing style. That is why no one can learn to write well by studying a book--the only way to learn is to *do* it. Practice will teach him, much better than you or I could, when to break up sentences, when to bring the reader up short, when to repeat, when to quit.

> For the rest of the week, work on rewriting the
> paragraphs in Exercise 4-D, p. 41. Use everything
> you've learned about nouns and verbs, modifiers,
> prepositions and sentence construction.

WEEK 11. We've worked on mechanics; now for content. The student has been learning to use some tools of the trade, applying them mostly to impersonal textbook exercises. Soon he will begin to apply these tools to his own thought and experience. Parts One and Two dealt with mechanics and technique. Part Three delves into perception and emotion.

Until now you've been a close supervisor of the student's work, a step-by-step guide in the progression from words to sentences. Your goal from now on should be to move away gradually as he works his way through the rest of the book. By that time, a young person should be able to do his own thinking, selecting, drafting and correcting down to the final revision. This is *not* to say that I guarantee a polished young prose stylist. Chances are the work will be quite uneven--it may take off and soar in some spots but crash land in others. All I hope to do (and all you, as instructor, *can* do) is provide some coaching, practical tips and applicable skills. Good writing ultimately depends on the writer himself, and no one else.

Monday
Compare the rewritten paragraphs from last week with the examples below. Point out that my versions do not constitute the one "right" way to do it; each of them only offers one of many variations. If your student made all the indicated changes in one way or another, he's very observant and a fast learner. If not, he's typical.

1.   After the game, we went to Pizza Haven, which was packed with noisy party-goers. The whole room blared with talk and laughter and electronic beeps from the arcade games. After ordering our favorite anchovy and Canadian bacon pizza, we buzzed over to the games. I was high scorer for that day on "Galactic Destroyers." When our number was called, Todd and I went to fetch our pizza at the window. After we ate, Mr. Jensen allowed us ten more minutes for games. Until somebody's little brother put his elbow in my eye, I had a great time.

concrete nouns
more detail
better verbs
opened sentence with prep. phrase or relative clause

2.   The day was warm and fresh-smelling. Tulips and daffodils bloomed along the sidewalk where we strolled, and children ran and shouted in the park while their mothers lounged on park benches. A little girl on her bike was speeding toward us. She didn't know how to ride very well. "Look out," Dad gasped--but it was too late. The bicycle bumped the jogger in front of us and knocked

descriptive adj.
sentence connection
concrete nouns
better verbs

him down.

> Read p. 43 and be ready to talk about it tomorrow.

Tuesday

If you like the Emily Dickinson poem you may wish to look up a volume of her poetry at the library. The point here is that she was able to accomplish so much with a single thought. We can imagine her sitting at her window one winter day, wrapped in a blanket and sipping a cup of tea. Out of that simple experience--with the help of a snowflake, the wind, a bank of low clouds--came a poem. While it's true that most people, especially young people, don't have the depth of perception needed to turn ordinary events into literary masterpieces, a beginning writer must understand that he has a wealth of material to write about. That well-worn excuse "But I never *do* anything," just won't wash. Every child does plenty, every day. The trick is to learn to *look* at those everyday experiences.

Discuss p. 44 with the student and try to assess his thoughts and feelings. These ideas may spark the interest of a few children, who will then be eager to try writing some poetry. The majority may be slightly encouraged, but still not wildly excited about writing. And there will always be some who say, in effect, "I don't like this, and you can't *make* me like it." Those skeptical few should be encouraged to hang in there for the next several pages and give it their best anyway--they may be pleasantly surprised.

With that, turn the page. Eager beavers may want to complete the Christmas poem on their own, but the foot-draggers may benefit from a cooperative effort. If this is the case, read through the material together and take turns contributing sensory impressions appropriate to the season. The will be required to write two poems on the given model. If you have time, it might be helpful and instructive for you to write a poem on your favorite season. Using the model, it's not difficult--try it!

> Read p. 44 and write a poem following the instructions
> for Exercise 1-A.

Wednesday-Friday

Ask the student to read his poem aloud. Locate and comment on at least two lines that appeal to you. If you wrote a poem, read it now and let him tell *you* what he likes about it. If you both write about the same season, it would be interesting to compare the aspects of the season that affect each of you. If some lines in the poetry seem weak (i.e., vague or uncertain), work together on making them stronger--which nearly always means making them sharper and more specific.

In my experience, most young writers are intrigued by poetry once they've actually written a poem; some are even excited by it. I would encourage them to go ahead and write a "collection" of seasons as suggested in 1-B, p. 45. If combining them in a booklet with illustrations seems rather "uncool" to teenagers, you may recruit an artistically-inclined younger child to draw or paint a set of illustrations. If a desired media, such as oil pastels, makes book-making impractical, the pictures may be mounted on a wall or tacked on a bulletin board with the accompanying poem. Use your judgment--if your student is even halfway willing, take the rest of the week to work on the poems. If, on the other hand, he shows no interest whatever, it may be best not to push. Give him the rest of the week off.

```
Write three more poems on the other seasons, following
suggestions for Exercise 1-B, p. 45.
```

Week 12. I am using poetry as a means of opening up the student's perception of experience, not as a subject in itself. Teaching poetry is outside the scope of this book, but if the student shows some interest in writing more poems, other books are available. One I can recommend is *Easy Poetry Lessons That Dazzle and Delight*, by David Harrison and Beatrice Cullinan (Scholastic, 1999). It's written for younger children (grades 3-6), but the information is ageless and the activities can be adapted.

Monday

Read season poems out loud and comment positively on any details you especially like. Then go over each line and check for weak spots. Pay special attention, once again, to *nouns* and *verbs*. Are they concrete and vivid? Are all the senses included?

```
Reread your season poems and change any lines you
believe could be better.  Make neat copies of two of
them. Read Example 1-C on p. 45 and write a color poem.
```

Tuesday

Writing about a color is an exercise in abstract concepts. Some literal-minded children may have a little trouble with this (after all, colors can't be smelled or heard), but the example given should fire up imaginations. Every student should write at least one color poem. If that one turned out reasonably well, ask him to pick a color that seems totally opposite and write a contrasting poem.

```
Write another poem about a color.
```

Wednesday

Discuss and revise color poems, remembering to look for strong sensory impressions. You may want to frame each poem with the appropriate color for display.

```
Copy your color poems. Then read all the poems on pp.
91-92 and choose the one you like best.
```

Thursday

Talk over the sample poetry and analyze the poem your student selected: How are the senses involved? What words are repeated? Can you see a structure or pattern? What is it? (For example, every line of the soccer poem begins with an action verb.) Exposure to these various forms may start creative juices flowing. Also note the *look* of the poems on the page. Poetry should be displayed in a way that accents the rhythm, but allows room for creativity in the arrangement of lines. Notice how the "Spring" poem is arranged in separate, centered stanzas like blossoms, and how the "Fog" poem appears to creep in one direction and then another.

A word about rhyme here--I love rhyming poetry, but I'm convinced that few young people have the skill or vocabulary to fully express their feelings in rhyme. Some of my students have argued with me over this, but none have changed my mind. By all means, let your writer experiment with rhyme on his own time, but since the purpose of *these* exercises is to explore sensory impressions, insist on free verse.

> Exercise 1-D, pp. 45-46: Write a poem on anything that
> can be experienced easily through at least four of the
> senses. You may use any form or pattern, but don't try
> to make it rhyme.

WEEK 13. Some children take to figures of speech like a duck to water (to use a cliché). Others don't get along with them at all, and their writing will not necessarily suffer from it. But a dash of simile or metaphor adds spice to prose, so even if your student doesn't care for this sort of word play, he should at least give it a try.

Monday
Discuss the poem written last week. From a distance of three or four days, should any lines or details be changed? Are the sensory images sharp and clear?

> Revise your latest poem and make a neat copy. Read
> "Figures of Speech" on p. 46.

Tuesday
Discuss the difference between literal images and figurative images. Does he understand what an "image" is? Do you? Read aloud the list of unfinished similes in 2-A; you'll find the clichés coming to mind automatically. Before turning the student loose on this exercise, brainstorm together on some fresh comparisons for "light" and "heavy": "Light as paper," "Heavy as a fruitcake," "Light as the brain matter of a blonde," etc. (Sorry, blondes. You know we make these jokes only because we're jealous.)

> Finish the first ten similes in Exercise 2-A, p. 47.

Wednesday

> Complete exercise 2-A, p. 47.

I'm allowing some extra time for Exercise 2-A because similes are difficult for most writers to compose; the clichés come too easily to mind. Try to think of a few comparisons yourself, and compare your comparisons with the student's.

Thursday

> Read about metaphors, pp. 47-48, and write a metaphor
> poem on <u>one</u> of the abstract concepts listed in 2-B.

WEEK 14

Monday
Take a few moments to discuss what a metaphor is, reviewing the section about metaphor on pp. 47-48. Many young people enjoy writing metaphor poems--did yours? Which does he feel more comfortable with, simile or metaphor? Why?

> Write another metaphor poem, choosing another of the
> qualities listed in 2-B, p. 48.

Tuesday

> Read about personification on p. 48 and complete
> Exercise 2-C, pp. 48-49.

Wednesday-Thursday

> Write two poems imagining yourself as a personified
> object (Exercise 2-D, p. 49).

WEEK 15. This week the "real" assignments begin. You will notice a pattern in most of the following sections: an introduction with practice exercises; one or more assignments in which the student writes from his own experience; revision; and a final assignment requiring the student to transfer his experience to an imaginary situation. Your role will be to oversee progress, help with revision, and remind the student of any principles and techniques he has forgotten.

Many of the following assignments will include independent reading in the *Wordsmith* book. Some students, especially those already inclined toward literature and literary pursuits, will catch on quickly; others may benefit from talking over the material with you. Use your judgment as to whether your student can both understand *and* apply the material on his own. If you're not sure, you may wish to go through Section 3 with him to see how he does.

Monday

> Read and reread pp. 50-51. Then fill out the chart on
> p. 51 (Exercise 3-A).

Tuesday
Any of these details could be on the chart:

Sound--roar of traffic, squeaky chair, "whoosh" of curtains, hum
   of projectors
Smell--diesel fumes, buttered popcorn, cigarette smoke
Taste--popcorn, diesel fumes
Touch (texture)--velvet upholstery, crunch of popcorn
Sight--concrete, skyscrapers, mirrors, gilt, carved wood, domed
   ceiling, wide screen

> Read p. 52, choose a place to describe, and complete
> the chart under Exercise 3-B.

Wednesday
Look over the completed chart on p. 52 and discuss whether anything should be added. If you're familiar with the place the student chose to describe, you may think of something he forgot, but

don't insist that he include all your suggestions--what impresses you about the place may have little meaning for him. On the other hand, don't let him sit idly by while you fill up the chart. If he "just can't think of anything," ask him to imagine himself in the place. It may even be possible to send him there with a notebook and pencil. Don't allow yourself to be stonewalled! All we are asking him to do is write down some perceptions of a place. We all have *thousands* of perceptions; the problem is sorting them out. The chart is a tool to help the writer think about and arrange the details that bombard his senses every day.

Once the chart is completed, he has some material to work with. You may wish to go over the guidelines together before he begins.

```
Carefully read the guidelines under ASSIGNMENT 3-A, pp.
52-53 and write a description, one to two double-spaced
       pages long.  Proofread and make corrections.
```

Thursday
We'll spend some time on revision next week. All you should do today is make sure the student has completed the assignment. If you have a chance this weekend, make a copy of the description for comparison later. Be advised that pencil does not photocopy well--if the assignment was handwritten, go over it in black ink for best results. (You may wish to make a copy of a first draft periodically, as it is sometimes instructive to gauge improvements between the initial effort and the finished product.)

WEEK 16. It's important that a writer learns to proofread, evaluate and correct his own work. In my opinion, many "professionals" never learned to do this properly in their youth, and their work shows it. This week the student will begin learning what revision is and how to revise.

Review Quiz #2 may be assigned any time over the next two weeks, perhaps on a Friday. Since the quiz addresses material we covered some weeks ago, make sure the student knows he can check back in the *Wordsmith* book to brush up on sentence constructions, nouns, verbs, etc.

Monday

```
Read pp. 53-54 (to ASSIGNMENT 3-B).  Then revise your
description according to Revision Checklist #1, p. 89.
```

Tuesday
Now it's your turn. If the description at this point is full of cross-outs and write-ins, that's promising--commend it. If you see a suspiciously neat paper, it means that the writer could find nothing to correct, which in turn means that he hasn't learned to evaluate or that he's just too good. We'll rule out the latter for now.

Remember, it's always best to start with the positives. Read the description and find things to like about it: word choices, details, organization. Then look carefully for weak spots, but avoid the word "But--"!

Review the assignment guidelines on pp. 52-53 and be sure that all are included. Then turn to Revision Checklist #1 on p. 89 and read the description once for each item listed. This is tedious work at the beginning, but as a young writer trains himself to look for these things, it becomes automatic. You may decide to take turns: you read watching for word choices, while the student checks sentence structure. When you find a place that seems to need correction, discuss it first, then write the agreed-upon changes between the lines.

Careful judgment is important here; keep in mind that you don't have to correct everything on the first assignment. If the revision goes on too long a sensitive artist may develop a persecution mindset and start making observations like, "You never like *anything* I do," or "I'm gonna have to rewrite the whole thing." Nobody enjoys seeing his work taken apart before his eyes, so tread gently. Concentrate on content first--if the description doesn't contain many details at all or doesn't convey a sense of emotional involvement, work on that. If content is not a problem, compliment the student on his evocative details and ask if sentences might be improved. *Don't try to fix it all.* Remember this book contains many more assignments and many more revisions.

```
      Make a final copy of the description you revised
         yesterday; proofread, and make corrections.
```

Tell him he's getting off easy: most writers don't settle for just one revision. Tolstoy revised *War and Peace* at least seven times!

Wednesday
Proofread the final copy and mark any minor corrections that should be made. Be sure to compliment the improvements and be specific about the details you especially like. "Good job" is not enough. If you were able to make a photocopy of the original draft, this would be a good time to compare the two and let the student see for himself how revision improved the piece. Keep both copies in the creative writing portfolio or binder. You may wish to attach a snapshot or drawing of the special place.

```
      Read Assignment 3-B on p. 54 and rewrite your place
                         description.
```

Thursday
Rewriting assignments gives the student a hint of the process of composition, the shifting of an idea and how that shift can be communicated with words. How well did he communicate an atmosphere of suspense in the rewrite? Compare with Example #9 on p. 93 and make some suggestions of your own.

```
   Read Assignment 3-C on p. 54-55 and make another chart
    listing details of the place you choose to describe.
   Write a first draft, using guidelines on pp. 52-53.  Do
    not use the words "I see," "I hear," "I feel," etc.
```

WEEK 17. Now we can begin to move a little faster. This week the student will complete one assignment and begin another, ideally with less help from you. He may still need some guidance and encouragement, so be available. (You may wish to scout around for some pictures of interesting places to use later in the week.)

Monday

> Review Revision Checklist #1 (p. 89) and read your
> description, marking any improvements you may need to
> make. Then go through your paper one sentence at a
> time and thoughtfully make those corrections.

Tuesday

Ask the student to read the description to you and then help you analyze it. Check to make sure that all guidelines are included. (Declaring "I feel" off limits may prove difficult for some, but they must learn that there are many ways to get meaning across. "This place wraps me in peace," or "The old excitement tingles in my fingers" are just as meaningful, and actually more effective, than "I feel peaceful (or excited).") When you both are satisfied--or exhausted--with the revision, stop.

> Type or print descriptions #2 and keep it.

Wednesday

> Read p. 55 Following directions under "Just Imagine,"
> find a picture (if you decide to use one), make the
> cart, and begin writing a one-page description.

Thursday

> Finish the description you started yesterday; proofread.

Friday

> Take a Review Quiz #2, p. 97 - 98.

WEEK 18. The "Just Imagine" assignments are given to help two familiar types: those who don't think they have any imagination and those who have plenty but don't know what to do with it. *Everybody* has imagination. Most of us (myself included) find it difficult to dream up stories on demand, but that's not what imagination means. Being able to recall feelings, thoughts and sensations of the past and recreate them on paper is an imaginative act. The purpose of the imagination assignments is to show the hesitant student how those same feelings, sensations and thoughts can be projected into a place he's never been.

On the other hand, some children have been writing about imaginary places for years --maybe even living in them. *They* need to learn that even the wildest flights of fancy must be grounded in concrete, sensory detail in order to come alive for the reader.

(*The Playmaker* is a novel set in Shakespeare's time, which involves the the theater, political intrigue and the Protestant Reformation. If that sounds interesting, it's available in paperback.)

Monday

> Revise your description of an imaginary place according
> to Revision Checklist #1, p. 89.

Tuesday

Read the revised description. Praise the details that impress you and try to find a least one spot where more detail would be helpful. Be sure that the student has included s some indication of how this place makes him feel--all the more impressive since he's never been there!

> Make a final copy of your description. If you used a
> picture, keep it with your description in the
> portfolio. Then read the top half of p. 56 and follow
> the directions in the "Try It" exercise.

Wednesday
The "framed" description will not be a masterpiece but it should be focused--a simple study of one or two objects seen through a picture frame. The student will be learning to narrow his field of vision while writing.

> Read Assignment 4-A, pp. 56-57 and write a "self
> portrait."

Thursday
Read the student's self-description. (Incidentally, I've found that girls tend to be critical of the way they look, while boys are either positive or non-committal!) In this type of exercise it's very easy to bog down in details, which, though important, are secondary to the overall expression of the face. A writer must learn to include only those details which support his main theme or themes. Check to confirm how the supporting details really *support*. What is it in this face that shows confidence, or hope, or friendliness? You may want to get out a mirror and take a look at *your* (the teacher's) face, define the overall expression, and discuss what features contribute most to that expression. You may discover that eyes, eyebrows and mouth are the most expressive part of the face.

> Make any revisions necessary in your "self-portrait"
> and copy it.   Then read Assignment 4-B, pp. 57-58 and
> decide what TV personality you will describe. Observe
> this person over the weekend and make a guidesheet
> answering the questions on p. 58.

WEEK 19

Monday

> Review guidelines and example on p. 58 and write a one-
> page description of a "public" person. Proofread.

Tuesday

> Reread your paragraph, think about it, and revise
> according to Checklist #1. Then make a final copy.

Wednesday
Did you catch that? The writer is revising without your guidance. This is worth trying to see what he can do on his own. Read the paragraph once it's in the final draft and be sure to compliment at least one specific detail. From now on, the decision to see draft copies before they are revised is up

to you, based on how much supervision you feel is needed. For each assignment, I will explain what I believe are the most important principles to grasp.

> Read ASSIGNMENT 4-C, p. 59, carefully and rewrite your description of the TV personality.

Thursday

> Read pp. 59-60 at least twice. Choose a subject for ASSIGNMENT 4-D, start watching, and decide what your subject will be doing in your description of him or her. You don't have to write the paragraph today, but make a guidesheet answering the questions on p. 58.

WEEK 20

Monday

I find that writing descriptions of family members is very difficult for children, because they don't know how to objectively "frame" someone they know well. For that reason, take time to discuss the notes he made last week. Be sure he's focusing on *one* (or at the most, two) attributes of the subject and picturing him or her at a particular moment in time. Focusing is an important principle that will probably need reinforcement periodically.

> Write a draft copy of your description, double-spaced, using information from your guidesheet.

Tuesday

> If possible, have someone read your description as suggested on p. 60. Then revise and write a final copy.

Wednesday

> Read Assignment 4-E on p. 60, choose another subject and write a first draft.

Thursday

> Use Revision Checklist #1 to revise Assignment 4-E.

WEEK 21

Monday

> Take Review Quiz #3 on p. 99.

The third quiz re-visits sensory poems to remind the student of sensory detail, and paragraph rewrites to help him on the road to independent revision. Take some time this week to go over the quiz and review the techniques of word choice, sentence structure and use of detail.

Tuesday

> Read the "Just Imagine" paragraph on p. 61 and make a guidesheet of details that describe your ideal friend.

Wednesday

> Write a draft description of your ideal friend, remembering to show what this person is like by what he or she does.

Thursday

"Show, don't tell" is a creative writer's mantra. We've been emphasizing this already in our descriptions, but by now it should be explicit. While it's okay to write, "Beth is very self-confident," the writer would do better to *show* Beth's confidence by what she says, how she walks, what she does, etc. If you don't see this in the Ideal Friend description, discuss ways to *show* the subject's personality.

> Revise your description, than ask a friend to read it and tell you if it sounds like a person they would like to know.

WEEK 22. Narrative is basic to creative writing. It's often what we think of as "story telling," although, as I will point out later, a narrative is not necessarily a story. When we ask for a field trip report or a "What I Did at Grandma's" paper we are asking in part for a narrative.

Monday

> Read p. 61 and write a paragraph telling how to make a sandwich.

Tuesday

If possible, ask the student to try making the sandwich he described (if someone can be induced to eat it). Are the directions easy to follow? Most important, are all the steps in order? If coming up with alternatives for the word "then" proves difficult, point out that the two suggestions given are prepositional phrases. Look at the list of prepositions on p. 19 and try to think of one or two phrases that might fill the bill.

> Read Assignment 5-A on p. 62 and list the steps of a job that you do regularly.

Wednesday

> Write a complete description of the job (at least one
> double-spaced page), then read over it carefully to
> make sure you included everything.

Thursday

If you have more than one student, give them the same assignment and ask them to exchange papers after writing their job descriptions. If they had to exchange chores for a day, would each be able to carry out the job using only the written directions?

> Read the "Just Imagine" paragraph on p. 62. Think of an
> imaginary place and write down general directions for
> how to get there. It might help to sketch a map, but
> don't let anyone else see it.

WEEK 23

Monday

> Write directions to your imaginary place in paragraph
> form. Read carefully and add any step or turn that was
> left out. Be sure to include warnings or details the
> traveler needs to know.

Tuesday

> Ask a parent or friend to draw a map based on your
> description.

Wednesday

Read the description and compare with the map. Pay special attention to sequence and determine if any intermediate "steps" are needed. Remember, even though this is an imaginary place, directions to get there should still make sense! If the paper does not include any description or sense of place, ask for more sensory details.

> Revise your directions (see Checklist #1) and make a
> final copy. Include the map in your portfolio.

WEEK 24. More on the importance of detail this week. The examples on p. 63 should demonstrate how detail makes all the difference between merely serviceable writing and memorable writing.

Monday

> Read p. 63 and write a first draft of Assignment 5-B.

Tuesday

> Revise yesterday's assignment with Checklist #1, p. 89.

This assignment asks the student to recount an ordinary occurrence drawn from memory. The resulting story should be a little vignette, a snapshot of family life. Watch again for detail. This is the first time I have asked for a quote, and it won't be the last. Direct quotes are one of the easiest ways to add freshness and immediacy to a narrative.

Wednesday

```
Read pp. 64-65 and follow directions in the "Try It"
                    paragraph.
```

Thursday

The subject of focusing is extremely important, for expository as much as creative writing. (Many a report, essay and research paper has failed for lack of focus!) If there's any confusion about the difference between paragraphs 1 and 2 on pp. 64-65, emphasize the point that paragraph #2 concentrated on just a few minutes out of an entire eventful day. We've structured sentences, now we're structuring entire assignments, centering the action.

Remember the "What I Did Last Summer" composition--the one that probably bored you both to tears while you were working through Part One? I'm not a gambler but I would lay almost any odds that the piece was boring because it was too general. That's why choosing an incident to write about for Assignment 6-A is crucial. It would be wise to discuss the incident with your student to make sure that it can be adequately told, with plenty of supporting detail, in two or three double-spaced pages.

```
Decide on a subject for Assignment 6-A, pp. 65-66.  Be
   sure to limit yourself to one incident, and make a
         guidesheet answering all the questions.
```

WEEK 25

Monday

```
Write the first draft of Assignment 6-A and proofread,
checking to make sure that all guidelines are included.
```

Tuesday

```
Read the paper aloud to yourself or someone who shared
  the experience with you. Consider any suggestions or
         add any details that you may have left out.
```

Wednesday

```
Carefully read "How to Revise" (p. 88).  Then revise
   your narrative according to Checklist #2, p. 89.
```

Because this is the first full-blown narrative writing assignment in the book, you should take part in the revision. Whether you decide to read the narrative alone and write comments in the margins or to review it with your student, the main thing to look for is overall structure. The incident described must be complete, with no obvious gaps or lack of supporting detail. It's quite common for a young writer to choose too broad a topic (in spite of all my warnings), start out like gang busters, reach the end of the second page and realize that he's not even halfway through. So he uses the last paragraph to win the game, finish out the season *and* receive the Most Valuable Player trophy at the Sports Banquet. His narrative will seem unbalanced, to say the least. If this is a problem in the finished narrative, re-emphasize the value of *focusing*. Instead of covering a whole tournament, concentrate on one decisive play in one pivotal game. Rather than "The Day We Went to the County Fair," tell about "The Scariest Ride of My Life." *Break the habit of generalizing.* If a student can move from the vague and general to the specific and concrete, his writing will improve at least 100%.

Thursday

```
Read and revise your narrative and make a final copy.
```

WEEK 26. The student should write another narrative, repeating Exercise 6-B (p. 66) and following the same schedule:

Monday. Decide topic and make guidesheet.

Tuesday. Write first draft.

Wednesday. First revision.

Thursday. Final revision and re-copy. (Or save copy work for Friday.)

WEEK 27. I've given so many suggestions in the "Just Imagine" paragraph on p. 67, it may be difficult for the student to choose just one--let him write two! If you feel he is mature or confident enough by now to follow through on his own work, assign a narrative to be finished by the end of the week and let him pace himself. If he still needs a little guidance, break down the assignment into increments similar to last week's schedule.

WEEK 28. Dialogue is sustained conversation, as opposed to a single quote or two. The section on dialogue is intended to help a student **listen** first of all, then **reproduce** what he hears. In addition, he will be required to **edit** what he writes, choosing the most important, telling, or characteristic words or phrases.

Monday

```
Read pp. 67-69 carefully, then write a conversation as
directed in the "Try It" paragraph on p. 68. Revise the
conversation according to "Try It Again," p. 69.
```

Tuesday

> Read pp. 70-71. Decide whom you would like to interview, choose a topic to discuss, make an appointment with him or her and write a list of questions to ask.

Wednesday-Friday

> Interview your subject, make a guidesheet answering the questions on p. 71, and write a draft of the interview.

The student should plan to interview someone he can talk to this week, say on Wednesday or Thursday. Go over his list of questions with him to make sure that they will cover the topic adequately.

If possible, the student should write his first draft the same day as the interview. Check the guidesheet before he begins to make sure all questions are answered.

If you read the draft copy, ask yourself these questions about the student's work: Is the "interviewee's" speech reproduced accurately (does it sound like this particular man or woman talking)? Are nonessential or peripheral comments edited out? Are supporting details and actions included? The interview should stick to one topic, and cover it fully.

WEEK 29. Either or both of the imaginative assignments of the next two weeks will fit well with any history topic you happen to be studying. The student will have to use solid historic fact as well as imagination to be plausible. Science topics lend themselves to these forms also: your student could "interview" a great scientist, or an amoeba, or write an exciting radio drama called "Attack of the Killer Virus."

Monday

> Read the "Just Imagine" assignment on p. 72. Decide on the person you would like to interview and write a list of 4-5 questions to ask him or her.

Tuesday

> Research your chosen character and write answers to the guidesheet questions on p. 71.

Wednesday

> Write a first draft of your interview.

Thursday

> Revise your interview and make a final copy.

WEEK 30

Monday
Read the imaginative interview with an eye to vividness of detail and sympathy with the character. Does your student seem to understand this person? If not, discuss what might have made him or her "tick," and how those motivations might be brought our in the interview.

```
Read pp. 72-73 and choose a narrative for a radio play.
```

Tuesday
I included the narratives on p. 73 to give the student a variety of material to work with, if you decide not to integrate the writing with science or history. Writing and taping a radio play could make an interesting group project to go along with this assignment.

Wednesday-Thursday

```
Revise your radio play and make a final copy.  If you
      like it, gather a few friends and record it!
```

WEEK 31. Changing point of view is often a liberating experience for young writers. It's also mind-stretching and fun. You might want to try it yourself!

Monday

```
Read p. 74 through the "Try It" paragraph; write a
     short description entitled "I Am A Pencil. "
```

Tuesday

```
Read through the "Try It Again" paragraph on p. 75 and
            rewrite the conversation as directed.
```

Wednesday-Thursday

```
Read Assignment 8, p. 75 and write the first draft of a
                 rewritten narrative.
```

WEEK 32
Monday

```
  Write a final draft of your rewritten narrative.
```

Tuesday

```
Read the "Just Imagine" paragraph on p. 76, decide on a
  scene to narrate, and write a draft from your first
                    point of view.
```

Wednesday

```
        Write draft from point of view #2.
```

Thursday

```
        Revise both scenes and make a final copy.
```

WEEK 33. I don't consider short story writing to be the epitome of all literary endeavors, but the concluding section of *Wordsmith* is a fitting climax to this book. Virtually all the techniques and principles of effective writing that we've studied thus far must be employed in a good short story, plus the invaluable discipline of structuring. The student should understand that he's about to embark on a big project which could take anywhere from two to four weeks.

Monday

```
                Read pp. 77-78.
```

Tuesday

```
    Reread pp. 77-78 and follow directions in the "Try It"
                    paragraph on 79.
```

Wednesday

Discuss the work the student did yesterday--would the news article, as he structured it, make a good story? Collaborate on adding a few made-up facts or rearranging elements to make the story more interesting, and discuss what the people involved might be like. Together you might develop fascinating fiction out of a bare-bones news article.

```
    Read p. 79 through the top half of p. 80 and fill in
            the story structure outline on p. 80.
```

Thursday

```
    Read p. 81, decide on a subject for your story and
                    write an outline.
```

Friday

```
            Take Review Quiz #4, p. 100.
        Again, the quiz addresses material long ago
        covered, but sentence and paragraph revision
                cannot be over-emphasized.
```

WEEK 34. This week the student will write a story on the subject he chose last week. Before he gets seriously into it, you should take a few minutes to discuss the story and how he plans to tell it. Look at his outline and try to estimate how many pages will be required to cover the material.. It's best to encourage a short short story for the first effort--embarking on a ten-page epic may prove to be discouraging for novices who find they've bitten off more than they can chew. But if he's determined to tell a particular story, let him tell it even if it runs to twenty pages.

Monday

```
          Read p. 82; write an opening sentence.
```

Tuesday- Friday

```
     Read p. 83 and write the first draft of your story.
```

WEEK 35. The revising schedule is up to you. Depending on length, a story could profit from three or four revisions, but by that time, of course, the paper is so marked up it's almost impossible to read. The ideal solution is putting the story on a word processor and running off a fresh copy for each revision. I would insist on two revisions for this first effort, with a few days between them. On pp. 85-86 of *Wordsmith* is an example of a first draft with revisions marked. You may want to look at this together.

WEEK 36. The student can make a final copy early in the week and rejoice in a job well done. Many young people are delighted to find that they can do this and, while they may not be ready to jump into their next story right away, they will be receptive to writing another one "sometime." Perhaps, depending on your schedule, you will have time to do that before school's out. At least, he's written an entire story--future writing assignments should be much less intimidating, and some of them may even be fun.

WHERE DO WE GO FROM HERE?

You're not through with this book yet! The guidelines and steps used to complete the assignments in Part Three will work for many creative writing assignments in the future. Here are some ideas for next year's projects:

DESCRIBING A PLACE
Describe a special vacation spot you visited last summer; write an advertisement for a resort area (whether you've been there or not); write a newspaper article modeled on a piece in the travel section of the Sunday paper; imagine and describe a medieval monastery, a space shuttle interior, Independence Hall, El Dorado, Heaven, etc.

DESCRIBING A PERSON
Picture a close friend at a special moment; write "family portraits" of everyone around the Thanksgiving table or Christmas tree; determine the character of a celebrity or world leader from his or her photo and write a description.

NARRATIVE
Write about The Time I Laughed The Hardest, The Happiest Day of My Life, The Time I Felt Sorry For My Mom (Dad, Sister, etc.), How to Play My Favorite game (real or imagined). Write a narrative about a news story as though you were present; write "I Was There When. . ." stories about famous historical events.

DIALOGUE

Plays are the thing! Write radio dramas, "readers' theater" stories, educational dialogues. Choose narratives from fables and folk tales, children's literature, even textbooks.

POINT OF VIEW

For a book report, describe the climax of the book from the POV of one of the characters. Imagine an issue or a news story from the POV of two people taking opposite sides. Record historic scenes from the POV of two participants (narrative). Write a conversation between a "pro" and a "con."

STORY

An Experience that Taught Me An Important Lesson; The Fear I Faced Down; A Special Moment with Grandma, etc. The student can branch out from non-fictional to fictional stories, often just by drawing from an actual event and changing the setting to another place and time. People have been learning the same basic lessons for ages, and will still need to learn them in space colonies or biospheres.

Essays and reports are not "creative" in that they don't deal primarily with subjective experience. But some creativity in expository writing is a big plus.

An **essay** is simply an exposition of the writer's view or opinion on any given topic. It can address any subject from world peace to mismatched socks. The appeal of an essay is always enhanced by some mention of the author's personal experience--narrative, sensory detail, and word images figure here. A student writing about "What I Wish People Would Understand About Christmas" could simply state that she doesn't like to see the spiritual significance of the holiday washed out. But the reader's interest would be engaged right away if she began her essay with a short narrative of an experience that showed her how Christmas was becoming over-secularized. In an essay entitled, "Love Is the Answer," one illustration of love in action is worth pages of nice platitudes.

For a **report**, you could assign the same tired stuff beginning "Ulysses S. Grant was born . . . " or you could ask your student to study a portrait of Grant and begin his biography with a description of the man portrayed. From there, the writer could relate some of the experiences that shaped the character shown in the face. Imagining himself on the scene when the Declaration of Independence was signed will give new freshness to an old story. Ask him to imagine the emotions of the participants, to describe the setting, to include a quote or two. Even science reports could be enlivened by personifying atoms or narrating the life story of a cell.

WRITING ALL OVER THE CURRICULUM

Creative writing can be applied in almost every school subject. Assigning a writing project for history, science, or art can provide more of that all-important practice as well as enhance learning. The enhancement works two ways: if a student doesn't like the subject, a creative writing assignment can help him "get personal" with it by approaching from a subjective slant. On the other hand, if he doesn't like writing, but enjoys the subject, it will give him a chance to practice writing skills on material that holds his interest. No matter what the assignment, the same rules-- clear word choices, effective sentences, use of detail and focus--will apply.

In addition to the ideas mentioned above, here are suggestions for incorporating creative writing into other areas of the curriculum. They are arranged from least demanding to most.

HISTORY

Homemade brochures: take pictures or buy postcards at an historic site. Use them to illustrate your own brochure, with captions, quotes, and interesting facts.

Write the history of an object seen in a museum.

Write letters or diary entries from the viewpoint of a character in a historical novel or story.

Create a newspaper from a historical time, including eye-witness accounts, interviews with famous people, editorials on issues of the day--a good group project.

Take a journey in your time machine: record events and conversations of a single day in the past and note the aspects of life that would be most difficult for you to adapt to.

Rewrite important documents in your own words.

Write a "What if..." story showing what might have happened if a particular event in history had turned out differently (I'll admit, the focus would be hard to maintain on this one, but it could be a great imagination-stretcher).

Choose a quality such as "tolerance," "patriotism," "dissent," etc. and write a metaphor poem about a character in history who exemplified that quality.

Write a dialogue or debate between two historical characters who held opposing views.

Write a physical description of a character in history from two opposing points of view (e.g., Abraham Lincoln during his visit to Richmond in 1865, described by a freed slave and a defeated southerner).

Write a review of an influential book (e.g., *Uncle Tom's Cabin, The Communist Manifesto, Common Sense*) as though you lived in the time it was written.

SCIENCE

Write personifications of simple science processes: "I am a . . ." (cloud, leaf, skin cell, etc.).

Write an imagined interview with a scientist of the past.

Write a radio play describing activities of the body, or any other scientific process.

MUSIC

Write short narratives inspired by program music (i.e., music that is supposed to describe something, like Beethoven's Sixth Symphony, Smetena's *The Moldau,* or Holst's *The Planets*).

Listen to a symphony and write a story suggested by the music. Each movement will represent a twist in the plot, suggested by changes in key, tempo, and dynamic.

Write sensory poems inspired by descriptive pieces, such as Vivaldi's *Four Seasons* or *Carnival of the Animals* by Saint-Saens.

Write imagined descriptions of Moussorsky's *Pictures at an Exhibition.*

Write a dialogue written to a quartet, trio or duet.

Write words to a piece with a recurring theme, such as Pachabel's *Canon* or Ravel's *Bolero*.
Write a radio play based on Tchaikovsky's *1812 Overture*.

ART
Write the thoughts of the people or animals depicted in a painting.
Write a dialogue between figures in an historical painting.
Write a poem inspired by an action painting; use lots of strong verbs and sensory details.
Describe the same scene from the opposing points of view of two figures in the painting.
Write a poem on feelings associated with an abstract work, including all the senses.
Describe the outstanding character traits revealed in a portrait (two of my favorite paintings for this
    assignment are John Singleton Copley's *Paul Revere* and John Singer Sargent's *Madame X*).
Describe a landscape painting as though it were the setting for two opposing fictional genres (such
    as a mystery novel and a romance, ghost story and a comic novel). Use words and details that
    emphasize the particular "slant" you wish to give the scene.

WRITERS, INC.--ORGANIZING A WRITERS' CLUB

Depending on your geographical location, the number of students in your area who might be
interested, and the availability of teachers or monitors, a Writers' Club can be good incentive for
young people practicing their skills. Of course, we know that lots of young people could care less
about practicing their skills, but the parents want them to, and if they see many of their peers in the
same predicament, they might take it with a little more grace. At the very least, a writers' club is an
opportunity to socialize, and socializing is what many 12-15-year-olds like best.

The members of an adult creative writing group typically make copies of all their writing projects
and distribute them to the other members for critique. A writers' club composed of young people
may do this occasionally, but their purpose is improvement, not publication. It's easier to have
them exchange papers with a partner for peer review. Some time during each meeting should be
set aside for this, with students swapping papers twice with different partners to get two different
points of view on their work. As I've mentioned before, peer-review can be instructive but isn't
always helpful for developing real skill--one should look to a teacher for instruction, not his peers.
The chief value of peer review is that students may be more motivated to do their best, but major
assignments should still be evaluated by a teacher.

The rest of the meeting (it's actually a class, but "meeting" sounds more fun!) could be taken up
with participation in a short exercise (many of the *Wordsmith* exercises are easily adaptable to a
group), some instruction or discussion regarding what they've read or written, and an assignment
for the next meeting. The club could meet weekly for a determined period, or monthly for the
entire school year. Once they've completed the regular *Wordsmith* assignments, many more
writing adventures await in the suggestions given on the last three pages of this book.

Round-robin stories make a good group activity: distribute a provocative opening paragraph to
each participant and ask them to write another paragraph in the story, then pass it on to the next
person to write a further paragraph, and so on. The next-to-last writer brings the story to a climax,
and the last will provide the falling action. Each member could begin with a different paragraph, or
use the same paragraph for everyone and see how widely the stories diverge. (This exercise won't
necessarily teach anything, but it's fun, and can demonstrate the unlimited possibilities of creative
writing!)

The Mysteries of Harris Burdick, by Chris Van Allstyn, is a great imagination starter. The book contains nothing but pictures, captions and titles--the reader must supply the story. Give every writer a copy of a different picture from which to develop his own story, or ask every member of the club to write a story on the same picture. Or, distribute pictures to the club as starters for round-robin stories.

GETTING INTO PRINT

Nothing can match the thrill of seeing one's own words printed out in black ink on glossy paper. Periodicals which publish writings by children are often under-funded and short-lived, but there are a few established mastheads. If your student has written a poem, story, essay or description that you're especially proud of, why not submit it for publication? You'll only be out a little postage and some time. Be aware that most periodicals are swamped with submissions--but they always publish some of them!

Many libraries keep a copy of *The Writers' Market* at the reference desk. This is a guide to periodicals, updated yearly, that contains information on hundreds of publications: editors' names, addresses, pay scales, and tips on what type of material to submit. Look at the "Children/Juvenile" and "Young Adult" chapters of the Consumer Periodicals section. Many of these magazines accept poems and stories from children (but don't pay much, if anything).

It's wise to write the publication first (or have your student write) and ask for guidelines. The editorial staff will mail a handout explaining the kind of material they're looking for and the format they prefer. This could save you some of that time and postage.

In addition, *Guideposts* Magazine sponsors an annual Young Writers Competition that awards big prizes and draws a huge response. Write them at 747 3rd Ave., New York, NY 10017 for details.

SUGGESTED ANSWERS FOR REVIEW QUIZZES

(Remember, these are for comparison only, except where noted otherwise.)

Quiz #2, pp. 97-98

I. Answers to #2, 7 and 10 should be close to the answers given here.
1. Jim slammed the ball.
2. Every week, Congress passes more spending bills.
3. We need volunteers to contribute to this cause.
4. During baseball practice with Tim, James lost his watch.
5. Watch for the lilac bush on the corner where you should turn.
6. Centerville Library boasts a great selection of children's books.
7. The technicians at Office Stop fixed the computer.
8. The telephone buzzed (or jangled, or whirred, or however your telephone
   sounds).
9. Mr. Brown crunched his cornflakes.
10. That scary movie terrified Gwendolyn.
11. Where there is life, there is hope.

II.   The summer sun burned our necks and made us sweat, so Howard and I decided
to go rafting. We launched our inflatable raft on the creek and climbed aboard.
After drifting with the cool current for a while, Howard spotted a flat brown
shell paddling toward us. Then a flat brown head stuck up out of it. "It's a
snapping turtle!" Howard exclaimed.
     "No," I laughed. "It's an alien space craft!" We hurled sticks at it until
it turned slowly in the water and swam away. That was a perfect summer day.

III.
1. Gray-green waves topped with foam sparkle on the ocean.
2. Over my head, seagulls cry and shriek.
3. The air is heavy with the smell of fish.
4. Wet, grainy sand squishes up between my toes.
5. The cherry Popsicle I bought from the ice cream wagon melts on my tongue.

Quiz #3, p. 99

III, 1. I love summer rainstorms. In the west, the sky gathers in a big black
frown and soon a wind from that direction cools the sweat on my arms and face.
Sometimes the storm rushes in, and my mother runs outside to take the laundry off
the line, yelling, "Jonah! Put your bicycle away!" Before long, big fat
raindrops are splatting on the hot sidewalk. Sometimes bullets of hail rattle on
the carport roof as we huddle under it for shelter. After the storm passes, the
whole neighborhood looks like it's been scrubbed.

Quiz #4, p. 100

I.
1. He half-skips as he crosses the street, whistling "Sunny Day."
2. Empty soda cans and candy wrappers surrounded the unmade bed.
3. Her shoulders slumped over the empty box, and she gave a long sigh.
4. Contentment cuddles next to me like a soft, warm blanket.
5. He strode toward me, shoulders back and eyes alert.

II, 2. Hank's knock rang on the door of the deserted warehouse with an empty
echo. Stepping inside, he felt a chill of fear on the back of his neck. An odd,
chemical smell from the right-hand corner made his nose tingle. He glanced that
way, but the corner was empty.